EXPLORE SIMPLE MACHINES!

WITHDRAWN

Anita Yasuda

Illustrated by Bryan Stone

More engineering titles in the **Explore Your World!** series

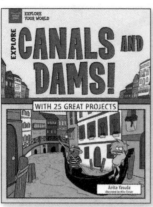

Check out more titles at www.nomadpress.net

Nomad Press
A division of Nomad Communications
10 9 8 7 6 5 4 3 2 1

This book was manufactured by Versa Press,
East Peoria, Illinois
August 2019, Job #J18-13170

ISBN Softcover: 978-1-61930-817-6
ISBN Hardcover: 978-1-61930-814-5

Educational Consultant, Marla Conn

Questions regarding the ordering of this book should be addressed to
Nomad Press
2456 Christian St.
White River Junction, VT 05001
www.nomadpress.net

Printed in the United States of America.

CONTENTS

Interested in primary sources? Look for this icon. Use a smartphone or tablet app to scan the QR code and explore more! Photos are also primary sources because a photograph takes a picture at the moment something happens.

You can find a list of URLs on the Resources page. If the QR code doesn't work, try searching the internet with the Keyword Prompts to find other helpful sources.

KEYWORD PROMPTS

simple machines 🔍

SIMPLE MACHINES!

5,000 BCE:
The Egyptians use a lever as a balance to weigh gold.

3,500 BCE:
Potters use wheels to shape their clay in Mesopotamia.

Prehistoric peoples use levers to dig and plant, and as oars.

4,000 BCE:
The Greeks use waterwheels to grind grain.

3,000 BCE:
People in North America use bows and arrows for hunting.

2,000 BCE:
People in the Middle East learn how to make lighter wooden wheels with spokes.

2,500 BCE:
The Egyptians use ramps to construct the Great Pyramid.

100–200 BCE:
The screw is used as a device to lift water and in other machines, including olive presses.

1,500 BCE:
People in Mesopotamia use rope pulleys to lift water.

500–1,000 BCE:
The Chinese invent the spinning wheel.

476 BCE:
Construction of the Great Wall of China begins. Many simple machines are used.

70 CE: Construction begins on the Roman Colosseum using simple and compound machines. When built, elevators will transport animals and props to the fighting arena.

581 CE: Construction begins on the Grand Canal in China. Some sections use ramps.

1450: Construction of Machu Picchu in the Andes Mountains of South America begins. Many simple machines are used.

1687: Isaac Newton publishes his three laws of motion.

100 BCE: The Romans build arches with the wedge-shaped key stone.

1853: The first commercial elevator goes into service.

2016: A Latvian company creates the largest Rube Goldberg machine.

1893: George Ferris builds his Ferris wheel for the World's Fair in Chicago.

1969: Engineers build the Saint-Louis-Arzviller inclined plane.

2019: One the world's biggest Ferris wheels will be the Ain Dubai.

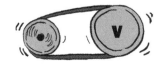

WHAT ARE SIMPLE MACHINES?

People have been using simple machines for a very long time. These machines don't have to be plugged in or turned on—they don't use electricity or gasoline. They work with muscle power. A simple machine is a tool that uses one movement to complete work. All of us use simple machines in our daily lives to make work easier.

Imagine the year is 2470 BCE. It's your first day on the job at the Great Pyramid of Giza. The desert sun bakes the quarry below. Wiping the sweat from your forehead, you pick up your chisel. You need to finish cutting this massive stone block. There's not a moment of rest for a worker such as you!

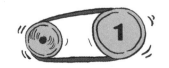

1

SIMPLE MACHINES!

The Great Pyramid is so large that it's made of more than 2 million blocks of stone! How did ancient people build such towering structures as the Great Pyramid? They had no bulldozers or backhoes or cranes. But they did have simple machines.

People discovered that simple machines gave them a mechanical advantage. These machines made it easier for them to get work done.

In science, the term "work" does not mean homework or chores. It means using a force to move an object. Turning on a light switch is an example of this kind of work. Opening or closing a door behind you or shoveling a snowy path are others.

There are six types of simple machines—the lever, inclined plane, wheel and axle, screw, wedge, and pulley.

Play some games to find out more about forces and motion! **Check out the videos on this website.**

KEYWORD PROMPTS
BBC guide what is force

Six Simple Machines

Lever: A long pole such as a stick on a fulcrum. It lifts loads up or down.

Shovels are levers that can help you move dirt.

Inclined plane: A sloped surface such as a slide at the playground. It connects a lower level to a higher level.

Ramps are inclined planes used to raise or lower a heavy load.

Wheel and axle: A wheel with a rod that turn together. It lifts and moves loads. The axle is the rod around which the wheel rotates.

Cars, school buses, and trucks need wheels and axles to roll.

Screw: An inclined plane or lever wrapped around a pole. It pulls one thing toward another.

Lids are screws that seal jar openings.

Wedge: An object with slanted sides ending in a sharp edge. It lifts or splits another object.

Zippers are wedges that fasten your coat.

Pulley: A grooved wheel with a rope. It changes the direction of an object.

School flags are raised by pulleys.

SIMPLE MACHINES!

engineer: someone who uses science, math, and creativity to design products or processes to meet human needs or solve problems.

crops: plants grown for food and other uses.

WORDS TO KNOW

Simple machines help people to pull and push. They can make it easier to lift objects. They also help to break apart or divide objects.

In North America, a Native American group called the Haudenosaunee, or Iroquois, are skilled engineers. Before European settlers came to North America, they used simple machines called digging sticks to plow the soil and plant crops such as corn.

The ancient world also used simple machines to build huge structures. Workers used many different simple machines to build the Great Wall of China. When completed, it stretched more than 13,000 miles long!

THE GREAT WALL OF CHINA

4

Compound machines are two or more simple machines working together to make tasks easier. There are a huge variety of compound machines, including bicycles, pliers, wheelbarrows, and scissors.

WHY DID THE SIMPLE MACHINE STOP WORKING?

It didn't have the energy!

The pedals and wheels on bicycles form cooperating wheel-and-axle systems, while the brakes are levers and the parts are held together with multiple screws. Pliers are constructed with multiple levers. A wheelbarrow is a combination of a lever and wheel and axle. Scissors consist of two pivoting levers and two wedges.

As you can see, people are still using simple machines. In fact, they are all around you. You can find them in your home, school, and park. They are in the games you play. You whizz down slides that are inclined planes and ride up and down on a lever called a seesaw. They are even in your mouth! Your teeth are wedges that you eat with.

In this book, you'll learn how simple machines work and what they do for you. You'll do lots of fun experiments and projects. Plus, you'll read some silly jokes and a lot of amazing facts. Let's find out more in *Simple Machines!*

⋅⋅ DID YOU KNOW? ⋅⋅⋅⋅

A simple machine only works if you supply the energy. Energy allows you to move objects. A knife will lie on a counter until you pick it up and push it through an apple. The knife then moves in the direction of your force.

GOOD ENGINEERING PRACTICES

Every good engineer keeps a design journal! In the first activity, you will make your own science and design journal. Scientists use the scientific method to keep track of experiments and engineers use the engineering design process to keep track of inventions.

As you read through this book and do the activities, record your observations, **data**, and designs in an engineering design worksheet or a scientific method worksheet. When doing an activity, remember that there is no right answer or right way to approach a project. Be creative and have fun!

Scientific Method Worksheet	Engineering Design Worksheet
Question: What problem are we trying to solve?	**Problem:** What problem are we trying to solve?
Research: What information is already known?	**Research:** Has anything been invented to help solve the problem? What can we learn?
Hypothesis/Prediction: What do I think the answer will be?	**Question:** Are there any special requirements for the device? What is it supposed to do?
Equipment: What supplies do I need?	**Brainstorm:** Draw lots of designs for your device and list the materials you are using!
Method: What steps will I follow?	**Prototype:** Build the design you drew during brainstorming. This is your **prototype**.
Results: What happened and why?	**Results:** Test your prototype and record your observations.

MAKE A SCIENCE AND DESIGN JOURNAL

SUPPLIES

* cereal box
* scissors
* brown paper bag
* white glue
* recycled paper (copy paper, envelopes, junk mail, graph paper)
* hole puncher
* dental floss
* needle
* magazines
* pencil crayons

Scientist Isaac Newton (1643–1727) kept a journal and manuscript full of observations. You can make a journal to keep track of what you read and discover in this book.

IMPORTANT: Ask an adult to help you with the needle.

1 Cut your cereal box so it opens like a book. Cut across the top and bottom, following the fold.

2 Cut the brown paper bag into two 6-by-8-inch pieces.

3 Apply white glue to the outside of the cereal box and attach the brown paper. Set to one side to dry.

4 From the recycled paper, cut journal pages to 5 by 7½ inches. You need quite a bit, enough to fill the cereal box cover.

5 Use the hole puncher to make three holes, about 1 inch in from the edge, on your papers. The holes go on the left of your journal.

PROJECT CONTINUES ON NEXT PAGE . . .

6 Put the paper inside your journal's cover. Take a pencil and mark where the holes should go on the cover.

7 Punch matching holes in the front and back covers of your journal.

8 Thread a needle with dental floss and push it through the holes in the paper and the cover. When you are finished going in and out of each hole, secure the dental floss by tying it.

9 Draw pictures of simple machines for your cover or cut out images from magazines and glue them to your cover.

ESSENTIAL QUESTIONS

Each chapter of this book begins with an essential question to help guide your exploration of simple machines. Keep the question in your mind as you read the chapter. At the end of each chapter, use your design journal to record your thoughts and answers.

? **INVESTIGATE!**

What are simple machines? What are they used for?

CHAPTER 1

ALL ABOUT FORCES

Moving a heavy bag of sand with your bare hands is a tough job. But what if you had a simple machine to help? You could push the bag up a plank of wood, pull it with a wagon, move it with a wheelbarrow, or lift it with a shovel.

What about snowboarding down a snowy slope? What tool are you going to use to get down the hill quickly and safely (besides a helmet!)? A snowboard, which is also an inclined plane! By changing the power, speed, or direction of a movement, simple machines make work easier.

To better understand how simple machines make work much easier, you need to understand forces. Let's take a look!

SIMPLE MACHINES!

FORCES

You don't have to be in a movie for the force to be with you. The world is full of them! A simple push or pull is a force. You push on a door to open it. You pull on a door to close it.

When you stand still, the pushing and pulling forces are balanced. This balance is called equilibrium. There is no movement because the forces are equal. But when forces are unequal, they are unbalanced, creating movement.

Tug of war is a fun game that is an example of the push and pull of forces. If you play tug of war against a team of equal strength, the rope does not move much. But if one team is stronger, the rope moves backward and forward until one team falls—the forces acting on the rope are not equal.

INVESTIGATE!

What is force? What is gravity? How do forces affect motion?

A CITY OF SIMPLE MACHINES

The stone city of Machu Picchu in Peru is an ancient city built with simple machines. It was built during the 1400s by the Inca, who controlled large parts of South America. Inca workers might have used a system of inclined planes and levers to build more than 200 buildings in Machu Picchu. Some archaeologists believe they used earthen ramps to move boulders from quarries to work sites. Some of these boulders weighed as much as 14 tons!

WHICH PUPPY IS GOING TO WIN AT TUG OF WAR? TUG OF WAR IS A GAME OF FORCE.

Imagine standing at the top of a snowy hill with your snowboard. Ready to try some jumps and tricks, you push off. You turn, twist, spin, and balance. How did you do this? With the help of forces! Forces cannot be seen, but they can move you forward and backward, up and down. They can change your direction, speed you up, slow you down—even stop you.

TRY THIS!

Conduct this quick experiment with a straw. Balance the straw on your finger until you find the straw's center of gravity. Don't allow it to tilt. You'll find that the straw can balance only when the force of gravity pulls equally on both sides. The straw falls when the force of gravity is unbalanced.

WORDS TO KNOW

friction: a force that slows down objects when they rub against each other.

orbit: the path an object in space takes around a star, planet, or moon.

mass: the amount of matter in an object.

newton: a unit used to measure the amount of force you need to move an object.

GRAVITY AND FRICTION

To move an object, simple machines must overcome two natural forces—gravity and friction. Gravity is a force everywhere in the universe. It keeps the earth in orbit around the sun.

On Earth, gravity pulls all objects with mass toward the planet's center. Mass is what makes up an object. You have mass. So do animals, trees, and buildings.

HOW IS FORCE MEASURED?

Forces are measured in newtons. One newton is equal to one-quarter pound—the weight of a quarter-pound burger. The measurement is named for Isaac Newton (1643–1727), a world-famous scientist. According to a story, Newton became interested in how and why things move after seeing an apple fall from a tree. He then wanted to know why the apple did not fall sideways or go up. Newton's observations led to his discovery of how gravity works.

PS Learn more about Isaac Newton and his inventions in this video.

KEYWORD PROMPTS

learnenglish Newton 🔍

Because of gravity, when you leap into the air, you're pulled right back down. Without gravity, everything—including you—would fly off into space.

Friction is also a force. Friction slows two objects down when they rub against each other, such as a toy car on a carpet or a sled on snow.

When you walk down the street or slide over snow on your snowboard, friction is always working to slow you down. Friction moves in the opposite direction from the object in motion.

Imagine trying to use ice skates on sand instead of on a smooth, icy surface. Not much fun! The sand slows you down and trips you up. Rough surfaces such as sand or grass tend to create more friction than smooth surfaces such as ice or concrete.

Can you think of ways to fight friction? If you said try harder, you're right! To move, you must push harder than the force of the friction. You could also apply a lubricant. In skiing, wax is used as a lubricant. The wax reduces friction between the skis and the snow. In skating, water is the lubricant. It reduces friction, allowing the skate blades to glide over the ice.

Friction is also a useful force. Without friction, lots of things you take for granted, such as walking, would be impossible. When you walk, friction grips the soles of your shoes. Without friction, your feet would just slide!

Let's take a closer look at the six simple machines that help us do all kinds of work. First up—levers!

? CONSIDER AND DISCUSS

It's time to consider and discuss: What is force? What is gravity? How do forces affect motion?

SCIENCE AND SKI RACING

Top skiers need to be fast. They rely on training, the best equipment, and wax. Skis can't move directly over snow. The snow under the ski forms a sheet of water, and this water slows the skis down. But wax helps skis glide and grip the snow. Wax does this by repelling water. Instead of forming a film, the water beads up like tiny ball bearings, allowing the skis to move easily over the snow. At the PyeongChang Winter Olympics in 2018, the American ski team had as many as 300 waxes to test on athletes' skis!

PROJECT!

TEST THE FRICTION

In this experiment, you will see if you can decrease or increase friction!

SUPPLIES

* science journal
* pencil
* baking sheet or tray
* books
* toy car
* timer
* cardboard
* sandpaper
* dish towel
* carpet

1 Start a scientific method worksheet and write a prediction in your journal answering the following question: Which material will be easiest for a toy car to move over and why?

2 Set up a gentle slope by placing a baking sheet at an angle on a book. Place the toy car at the top of the baking sheet and let it roll down. Use a timer to record the time.

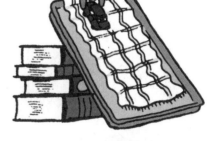

3 Repeat the experiment by placing different materials, such as cardboard or a dish towel, one at a time, on the baking sheet and letting the car roll down.

4 Write down your observations and results in your science journal. Which surface has less friction?

5 Create a bar graph based on your results. Check out how to make one on this website.

KEYWORD PROMPTS

NCES kids charts 🔍

TRY THIS! Set up your slope. Get a marble, ice cube, stone, and piece of wood that are roughly the same size and weight. Which object do you think will move fastest and why? Write down your prediction and test your idea. (Make sure you wipe off the tray after you test the ice cube.)

BALANCE CHALLENGE

A mobile is a piece of art with objects dangling from strings. All parts of a mobile need to stay balanced. Try to balance different objects from a mobile.

IMPORTANT: An adult must help with the wire cutters!

1 Bend a wire coat hanger to make a circle. Ask an adult to snip off the hook with wire cutters. Wrap yarn around the wire circle to completely cover it.

2 Tie four pieces of yarn, each 15 inches long, to the circle. The strings need to be evenly spaced. Gather the ends of the yarn together at the top.

3 Hang the mobile from a low hook and adjust the yarn strings to make it balance.

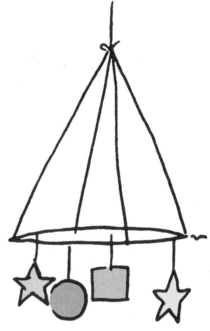

4 Select objects to tie to your mobile with yarn. If the mobile does not balance, keep experimenting with the objects until you can balance the mobile.

THINK ABOUT IT! When the mobile is level and balanced, what must be true of the forces acting on it? What about when the mobile is unbalanced?

CHAPTER 2

LEVERS

It's a warm summer day, and you're up at bat. Crack! Nice hit! Dirt flies as you race to first base. You're safe! When you play baseball, you use simple machines. A baseball bat is an example of a lever. You use levers when you throw a baseball, stand on your tiptoes, and nod your head.

You eat with levers—knives and forks. You turn on lights with a switch—another lever. Surgeons even use levers to control tiny robots that operate on people! And the keys of a piano? Also levers!

? INVESTIGATE!

How do levers change the strength of a force?

SIMPLE MACHINES!

lever: a simple machine made of a rigid bar that pivots on a support, called a fulcrum.

pivot: the fixed point—the fulcrum—supporting something that turns.

load: the object you are moving in your work.

bar: the part of a lever that balances the weight of an object and applies the force to move that object.

effort: the force that is used on a simple machine to move the load.

WORDS TO KNOW

A lever is a bar that turns on a pivot to move things. It's easy to see why levers are one of the most common simple machines.

A lever has four main parts that work together—load, bar, fulcrum, and effort. A seesaw is an example of a lever. When you and a friend sit on a seesaw, one moment you're on the ground and in the next you're in the air. What fun!

The load is what is lifted. When you are up in the air, you are the load. The bar is the plank that you sit on to move the load. The center of the seesaw is the fulcrum. The fulcrum allows the bar to change direction. The effort is the energy put into lifting something. That's your friend sitting on the other side, closer to the ground.

HOW LEVERS WORK

Imagine that you are on a seesaw with a friend. This friend weighs more than you. Where should you sit on the seesaw to lift this person?

Watch this video about levers. What does it tell you about where you should sit?

KEYWORD PROMPTS

YouTube lever math

There are three main types of levers—first-, second-, and third-class levers. The location of the load, fulcrum, and effort is different for each type of lever. And each type of lever is used for a different job. Let's take a closer look.

FIRST-CLASS LEVERS

A first-class lever has the fulcrum between the load and the effort. Imagine pulling out a nail with a hammer. When you use the claw of the hammer, the lever lifts the nail out. The head of the hammer is the fulcrum. You, pushing down on the handle, are the effort.

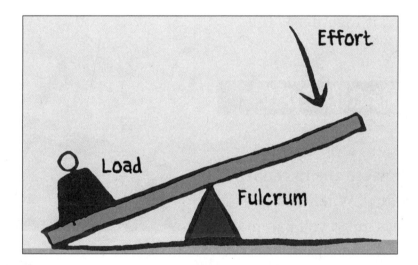

First-class levers are all around us. What do you reach for when you want to cut out something? Scissors! The fulcrum is where the two blades connect. The effort is you squeezing the blades and the load is the paper.

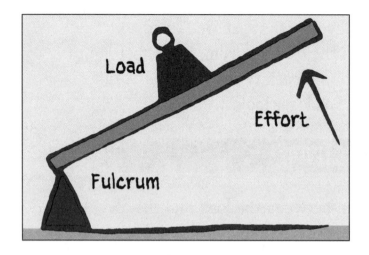

SECOND-CLASS LEVERS

A second-class lever has the load between the fulcrum and the effort. The load moves in the same direction as the effort.

A nutcracker is a second-class lever. When you squeeze the handles together, your force makes the nut crack. A stapler is also a second-class lever. The lever is the top of the stapler. The part of the stapler that holds it together is the fulcrum.

THIRD-CLASS LEVERS

A third-class lever has the effort between the fulcrum and the load. When you use a third-class lever, you can make an object go faster and farther.

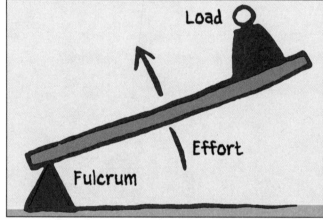

THEN & NOW

THEN: Ancient Roman doctors used levers to set bones and pull teeth.

NOW: Surgical robots are made with tiny levers that copy the movements of third-class levers in the human body, such as the wrist.

A baseball bat is a third-class lever when you use it to strike a ball. The arm you use to swing that bat is also a third-class lever. Your elbow works as a fulcrum. The muscles in your arm are the effort and the ball is the load. You also use a third-class lever each fall to rake leaves.

linkage: a link that connects two or more levers together.

International Space Station: a massive space station orbiting Earth where astronauts live, conduct experiments, and study space.

WORDS TO KNOW

WORKING TOGETHER

Sometimes, linkages join levers together. A linkage connects two or more levers together. When one lever moves, its motion is passed on to the next lever, and so on.

Have you ever played the game Pass the Squeeze? In this game, a group of people hold hands in a circle. When someone squeezes your hand, you squeeze your neighbor's hand, and so on, until the squeeze travels all the way around the circle.

CANADARM2

The Canadarm2 is a 58-foot-long robotic arm that works as a third-class lever. The robotic arm is attached to the International Space Station.

Learn how the Canadarm2 works by playing this game!

KEYWORD PROMPTS

CSA Canadarm2 simulator

SIMPLE MACHINES!

shaduf: a water-lifting device.

WORDS ⊚ KNOW

Linkages are a lot like this game. They pass movement from one part of a machine to another.

Machines that use linkages are all around you. Your bicycle uses linkages, for example. When you squeeze the brake lever, a series of linkages sends the force to the brakes on the wheels. Now that's working together!

LEVERS IN HISTORY

Levers have been making our lives easier for a very long time. For example, by 3000 BCE, people were settling in cities between the Tigris and the Euphrates Rivers in an area known as ancient Mesopotamia. Today, this is part of Iraq. Farming was important to people in Mesopotamia, and they used a first-class lever called a shaduf to lift water.

To work the shaduf, a worker pulled on the rope until the bucket reached the water. Water then filled the bucket. To lift the heavy bucket, the worker let go of the rope. A weight on the opposite end of the lever arm lowered to the ground and the bucket rose up.

Workers in ancient Egypt, Greece, and Rome also used levers to move stones into place. They pushed wooden rods or the trunk of a tree under the stone they wanted to move.

The workers then pushed down on the rod. The rod transferred the energy to the stone, making it move. Workers had to repeat this many times until the stone was in the correct place.

DID YOU KNOW?

In many parts of the world, farmers still use shadufs to lift water by hand. A shaduf can raise about 600 gallons of water a day.

MEET ARCHIMEDES

Archimedes (c. 287 BCE–c. 212 BCE) was a Greek engineer and scientist. He proved that the longer the lever arm, the less force was needed to move an object. "Give me a lever and a place to stand," he said, "and I will move the earth." Archimedes was born in Syracuse, Sicily, then a part of Greece. He invented many new tools and machines. He is said to have created a water pump that looked like a large screw. It raised water from rivers to fields. The device, called an Archimedes' screw, is still used to pump water. Archimedes created other inventions to use in war to protect Syracuse from Roman invaders. For example, he worked on the city's catapults. They fired stones and logs at invaders. He also invented a crane-like machine that used a lever and pulleys. Workers extended the crane's arm over the city's walls. Then, a pulley attached to the crane released rocks onto Roman ships, destroying them.

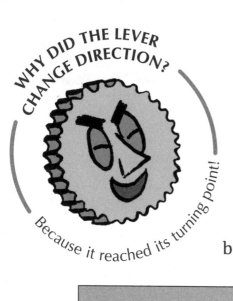

WHY DID THE LEVER CHANGE DIRECTION?

Because it reached its turning point!

Throughout history, the lever was also part of a weapon that could hurl objects a great distance—the catapult. A catapult worked like a giant slingshot. The arm of the catapult was held down with a rope. After soldiers placed a large boulder at the end of the arm, they cut the rope. The lever arm sprang upward, hurling the boulder at the enemy.

Without the lever, human history might have been much different! In the next chapter, we'll take a look at inclined planes, another important simple machine used for all kinds of things.

CONSIDER AND DISCUSS

It's time to consider and discuss: How do levers change the strength of a force?

FIRST-CLASS LEVER

First-class levers make lifting objects easier. Try this experiment to understand how a first-class lever works.

SUPPLIES

* modeling clay
* 12-inch ruler
* 2 cupcake liners
* tape
* bag of hard candies
* science journal
* pencil

1 Roll a piece of clay into a ball for the fulcrum. Place it on a table. Tape one cupcake liner to each end of the ruler. Rest the ruler on the clay ball like a seesaw. Fill the cupcake liner on the left with candies.

2 Start a scientific method worksheet and write a prediction in your science journal. How many candies will you have to place in the cupcake liner on the right side to balance the seesaw?

3 Begin placing candies in the cupcake liner on the right. Compare your results with your prediction.

DID YOU KNOW?

When you pull out a nail, a hammer is a first-class lever, but when you hit a nail, the hammer is a third-class lever. The fulcrum is the end of the handle. You, swinging the hammer down, are the effort and the hammer head is the load.

TRY THIS! Empty the cupcake liners. Move the clay ball a little closer to the cupcake liner on the left. Repeat the experiment above. Next, move the clay ball next to the cupcake liner on the left. Repeat the experiment above. Write down your observations.

SECOND-CLASS LEVER

Can you use a ruler to move a heavy object? Try and see. In this activity, turn a ruler into a second-class lever.

1 Which do you think will lift the can more easily, two of your fingers or the ruler? Start a scientific method worksheet and write your prediction in your science journal.

2 Try to lift the can with two fingers. Record your results in your science journal.

3 Use the elastic band to secure the can to one end of the ruler. Place the ruler on a table with 1 inch of the ruler hanging off the edge. The other end of the ruler is the fulcrum.

4 Using the same two fingers, lift the end of the ruler. Write down your observations in your science journal.

TRY THIS! Move the can closer to the center of the ruler. Repeat the experiment. Next, move the can until it is next to the table edge. Repeat the experiment again. Write down your observations.

CHOPSTICK CHALLENGE

When two chopsticks are used together, they work as a first-class lever. To use chopsticks, hold them at the top between your thumb and index finger, middle finger, and third finger. Your index and middle fingers control the chopsticks.

1 Make two equal teams. Give each team one empty bowl, one bowl with 10 sugar cubes in it, and one pair of chopsticks.

2 Ask an adult to say, "Go." Each person takes a turn using the chopsticks to move sugar cubes from one bowl to another. The first team to have all its players complete this challenge wins.

THINK ABOUT IT! You have to press only lightly on the chopsticks because a first-class lever takes a small movement and makes it bigger.

THEN & NOW

THEN: Heron of Alexandria (c. 10 CE–c. 70 CE) described the first vending machine. Water flowed from the machine when a coin fell onto a pan, lifting a lever.

NOW: Some vending machines still use levers. Once a coin is put into a gumball machine, it presses on a lever, allowing the knob to be turned.

MAKE A JUMPING JACK

A jumping jack is a puppet that moves with strings. The arms and legs of the puppet work as second-class levers. Try this project to see how it works.

SUPPLIES

* cereal box
* pencil
* scissors
* hole puncher
* 4 brass fasteners
* string
* colored markers

1 Flatten and cut open the cereal box. With the inside of the cereal box facing you, cut out one body rectangle and four smaller arm and leg rectangles.

2 Using the hole puncher, make two holes near the top of each arm and leg rectangle and a hole in each corner of the body rectangle. Look at the picture for guidance.

3 Line up the lower holes on the arm rectangles with the upper holes on the body. Secure with fasteners. The arms are now in place. Loop a piece of string through the top holes. Attach the legs the same way. Loop another string through these top leg holes. Tie a long piece of string to connect the top and bottom strings. Let the extra string hang down.

4 Color your jumping jack with a silly outfit. Pull down on the string and watch your toy move!

TRY THIS! How could you design your puppet to move its hands and feet? Sketch your ideas in your science journal and try them out.

CHAPTER 3

INCLINED PLANES

When it comes to having fun on a skateboard, ramps are very important. Ramps allow skaters to get big air and do cool tricks. All of these ramps are inclined planes.

Inclined planes are all around you. Slides, stairs, and escalators are inclined planes. Most public buildings and schools have ramps to allow people in wheelchairs and scooters to access them.

 INVESTIGATE!

How do inclined planes help people move objects?

inclined plane: a sloped surface that connects a lower level to a higher level.

skeleton: a winter sport in which a driver rides headfirst down a track on a sled.

WORDS ⊙ KNOW

An inclined plane is a flat surface with one end higher than the other. People use the inclined plane to move between areas of different heights.

A road can also be an inclined plane. Imagine walking straight up a mountain side. Whew! That would be tough. You use less effort if you take a winding road—which is an inclined plane—up the mountain. An inclined plane splits gravity into two smaller forces. So when you walk up a winding road, you go forward and up. You travel farther, but you use less effort.

SPORTY INCLINED PLANES

Athletes use inclined planes in lots of different sports. Downhill skiers use the natural incline of a hill to reach the bottom quickly. Sports such as bobsledding and ski jumping use inclined planes built by people to go faster and jump farther.

In a sport called skeleton, athletes lie on sleds about the size of a doormat. They hurtle headfirst down an ice track. And snowboarders use inclined planes for doing incredible, high-flying tricks.

The largest skateboard ramp in world was built in 2006 in San Diego, California. It's called the MegaRamp and is the length of several football fields. **Check out the world's largest skateboard ramp here!**

KEYWORD PROMPTS

NYT Burnquist video

The 2018 Winter Olympics introduced the new sport of big air snowboarding. Riders must drop down a 150-foot ramp. Imagine being flung into the air, tumbling and twisting, before touching down on the incline. The landing is yet another ramp that extends for hundreds of feet to slow riders down.

It's not only a challenging sport, but also a challenge to build for. Engineers must first look at the natural features of an area. Then, they carefully figure out the incline of the slope to allow athletes to perform their jumps and landings safely.

SIMPLE MACHINES!

switchback: a road that zigzags up a steep hill or mountain.

WORDS TO KNOW

A CHALLENGE!

Roads are often built with inclined planes because it's not possible to drive straight up a steep hillside or mountain. So, engineers design roads that wind their way to the top and back down.

What's the world's most challenging road? It could be the Stelvio Pass in the Italian Alps. At 9,045 feet, it is one of the highest roads in Europe. The Stelvio Pass has 48 narrow, hairpin curves. These curves are called switchbacks because they zigzag back and forth. It would be impossible for a car to climb the steep mountain without these inclined planes. Even so, drivers can't always see the oncoming traffic!

THEN & NOW

THEN: Not long ago, people using wheelchairs were unable to enter many public buildings in the United States because the buildings did not provide ramps.

NOW: In 1990, a new law—the Americans with Disabilities Act—was passed. It stated that all new construction in the United States must include a wheelchair ramp for easy access.

funicular: a type of mountainside railroad that uses cables attached to pulleys to move the train cars up and down.

WORDS to KNOW

Engineers also build inclined railways—called funiculars—to tackle steep inclines. In a funicular, a cable pulls a railroad car up a steep incline. In 2017, the steepest funicular in the world opened in Switzerland. It climbs more than 2,400 feet in about four minutes. Each of the four train cars is round. The cars always remain level because the round design lets them adjust to changes in the incline.

·· DID YOU KNOW? ·······

The world's longest staircase runs alongside the Niesen railway in Switzerland. It has 11,674 steps, rising 5,475 feet in 2 miles! Once a year, people can hike the staircase as part of the Niesen Run. Would you want to do this run? The ramp still exists today.

Watch a video to learn more about the world's steepest funicular in Switzerland.

KEYWORD PROMPTS

→ YouTube steepest funicular abb 🔍

canal: a long waterway made by people that moves water or is used for transportation.

trade: the exchange of goods for other goods or money.

lock: an enclosure in a canal with gates at each end used to raise or lower boats as they pass from one level to another.

Egyptologist: a person who studies the ancient history and culture of Egypt.

WORDS TO KNOW

WATER TRANSPORTATION

Waterways such as rivers and canals have been important to us for thousands of years. People use them to travel from one place to the next and for trade.

But what if there is a big difference in water levels between two bodies of water, blocking ships and boats from moving forward? To solve this problem, engineers invented the lock. A lock is a chamber with gates at either end. After a boat enters a lock, a gate closes behind it. The water level within the lock is then raised or lowered to match the height of the next body of water.

What does this have to do with inclined planes?

THE PYRAMIDS

Ancient Egyptians used inclined planes to build the pyramids. The largest pyramid in the world is the Great Pyramid of Giza, which contains more than 2 million stone blocks. Each block weighs between 2½ and 15 tons! How was the Great Pyramid built? Egyptologists do not yet know but have many different ideas. Maybe the ancient Egyptians used earth and mud bricks to make ramps. Maybe there was more than one ramp per pyramid. Or maybe they built ramps that spiraled around the pyramid as it was built. We are still figuring out the mystery!

Some canals were designed with inclined planes to move boats between different water levels. For example, China's Grand Canal stretches more than 1,200 miles—with parts of the canal dating back to the sixth century BCE. Sections of the canal have large, stone ramps called slipways. Workers once pulled ships up or down the slipway with ropes.

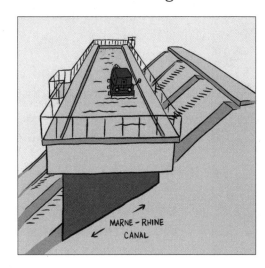

MARNE – RHINE CANAL

Modern engineers still use slipways on canals. The Saint-Louis-Arzviller is an inclined plane that is part of the Marne-Rhine Canal in France. It raises or lowers boats 147 feet. Before the plane was built, it took a ship up to 13 hours to complete the trip through a series of 17 locks. After the plane opened, it took ships only four minutes to be raised or lowered!

Inclined planes offer important solutions to all kinds of engineering challenges! In the next chapter, we'll take a look at a simple machine that is often found on an inclined plane—a wheel and axle!

·· DID YOU KNOW? ······

In ancient times, armies built inclined planes called siege ramps. These ramps made it possible for armies to haul heavy equipment to the tops of high walls. In 73 CE, Roman soldiers built a huge siege ramp using thousands of tons of dirt and rock to attack the hilltop Jewish settlement of Masada. The ramp still exists today.

? CONSIDER AND DISCUSS

It's time to consider and discuss: How do inclined planes help people move objects?

ICE CREAM SCIENCE

Science can be delicious! See how an inclined plane can help you make ice cream.

1 Pour the milk and vanilla into a measuring cup. Pour the sugar into the small plastic bag. Slowly add the milk and vanilla to the sugar. Carefully seal the bag and squish it to mix the ingredients.

2 Place the ice, the salt, and the sealed bag with the sugar mixture in the quart-sized plastic bag. Wrap the bag in a sheet of newspaper, place the wrapped bag in the coffee can, and put the lid on the can.

3 Set up an inclined plane with the board and books or boxes. Roll the can down the board over and over, until the mixture hardens. This will take about 15 minutes.

4 Open the can and take the bag out. Enjoy your ice cream!

TRY THIS! How did your inclined plane help to mix the ingredients? Change the angle and the length of your inclined plane or repeat this experiment without the inclined plane and compare your results.

SUPPLIES

* ¼ cup whole milk
* ¼ teaspoon vanilla extract
* 1 teaspoon sugar
* Ziploc plastic sandwich bag
* 2 cups ice
* ½ cup rock salt
* Ziploc quart-sized plastic bag
* newspaper
* metal coffee can with lid
* wooden plank or ironing board
* books or boxes

MINI GOLF CHALLENGE

Golf course engineers use inclined planes to create challenges for golf players. Learn how this works.

1 Cut out two large rectangles from the cardboard box for your inclined planes. The measurements are up to you.

2 Place the first cardboard piece at a low angle by propping it up with one of the objects (book, box, container) from the supplies list.

3 Join the second cardboard piece to the first with masking tape at the top of the slope. Prop it up so that it is higher than the first slope. Place the cup on the floor right behind the highest slope. This will be your hole.

4 Stand back a few feet from the first inclined plane with your  toy putter and ball. Try to hit the ball into the cup.

5 Write down your observations and results in your science journal. Based on your results, change your course. You may need to adjust the angle of your slopes, for example.

TRY THIS! Add more elements, such as obstacles, a tunnel, or more inclined planes, to your golf course!

SUPPLIES

* large cardboard box
* scissors
* books, boxes, plastic containers
* masking tape
* plastic cup
* plastic toy golf putter
* plastic golf ball
* science journal
* pencil

SKI SLOPE CHALLENGE

Create a ski slope in your kitchen. Will the angle of your slope affect the speed your racer travels? Try this activity and see.

SUPPLIES

* 2 popsicle sticks
* tape
* thick paper
* scissors
* plastic tray
* 6 to 10 books
* a smartphone or stopwatch
* science journal
* pencil
* an assortment of weights, such as large and small batteries

1 Arrange the popsicle sticks lengthwise and tape them together to look like a pair of skis. Draw a figure on heavy paper to ride on the skis. Tape it to the skis so that it is upright.

2 Place the tray on a book to create a ramp. Set the ski racer at the top of the tray.

3 Ready your timer and let go of the racer. Write your results in your science journal.

4 Make the ramp steeper by adding one book at a time. Repeat steps 2 and 3.

TRY THIS! Did the height of your ramp affect the speed? If so, why do you think this was? Add small weights to the popsicle stick skis. Write a prediction in your science journal. Do you think weights will change your results? Try and see.

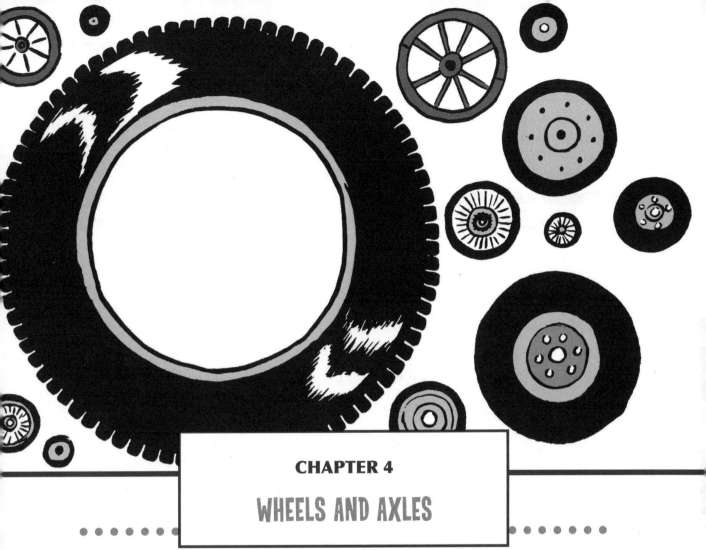

CHAPTER 4

WHEELS AND AXLES

Think about what life would be like without wheels and axles. No cars or trucks, no skateboards, bicycles, go-karts, or scooters, no pencil sharpeners, doorknobs, or screwdrivers! Wheels and axles are a pretty important part of our everyday lives.

A wheel and an axle are two objects joined together at their center. When one rotates, the other does, too. Wheels and axles come in lots of shapes and sizes.

INVESTIGATE!

How is force transferred between the wheel and the axle?

SIMPLE MACHINES!

·· DID YOU KNOW? ··········

Wheels belong to the lever family. A lever that moves all the way around in a circle is called an axle. The center of an axle is the point where the fulcrum used to be.

Can you imagine a construction team moving heavy objects before the invention of the wheel and axle? No bulldozers were there to help. To move heavy objects, you had to push or pull. You could also haul objects on rollers.

More than 4,000 years ago, builders in Europe and the Middle East began building huge stone monuments. Some archaeologists believe that workers used rollers to move these stones. The rollers acted like wheels. Rollers worked well to move heavy objects, but it was a slow process. Workers had to keep moving rollers from the back to the front of the object they were moving.

By 3500 BCE, Mesopotamians were moving heavy objects on sleds. At the same time, they began using wheels to spin pottery. Later, they joined large wooden discs with a central bar called an axle to create wheels.

spokes: bars or wire rods connecting the center of a wheel to the outside rim.

chariot: a two-wheeled, horse-drawn vehicle from ancient times, which was used in battle and in races.

WORDS TO KNOW

EARLY WHEELS

The first wheels were heavy and solid. They were made entirely of wood. The earliest example of a wooden wheel comes from Slovenia. In 2002, archaeologists were exploring marshes in Slovenia when they found the wheel. The wheel had a square hole in the center for an axle. Tests showed that the wheel was about 5,000 years old! Archaeologists believe that the wheel belonged to a cart.

From 2000 BCE, people began cutting crescent-shape holes into wooden wheels to make them lighter. Next, came wheels with spokes. The ancient Egyptians enjoyed hunting and used chariots to chase after wild animals. These chariots needed to go fast. Spoked wheels were much lighter and faster than solid wheels.

In 2016, archaeologists dug up a 3,000-year-old wooden wheel in Britain. **Watch a video to learn more about the wheel here.**

KEYWORD PROMPTS

Guardian bronze age wheel

41

POTTER'S WHEEL

The earliest wheels were used to spin thread, grind grain, and make pottery.

Around 3500 BCE, the Mesopotamians began using a round, spinning plate to make pottery. The potter placed a lump of wet clay on the plate and turned it by hand. As the plate spun around an axle, the potter molded the wet clay into an object such as a bowl.

Eventually, potters improved the potter's wheel so that it could be turned by foot. A heavier wheel rested on a smaller stone wheel and an axle joined them together.

THEN & NOW

THEN: An assistant turned a pottery wheel by hand while the potter shaped the clay.

NOW: Most pottery wheels are powered by electric motors.

The potter kicked the smaller wheel while molding the clay on the larger wheel above. By using wheels, potters could make objects faster and use less effort.

WATER WHEEL

In the past, humans and animals powered machines. Around the first century BCE, the ancient Greeks began using the water wheel to use the power of water.

These wooden wheels had buckets attached to the rim. The Greeks placed the wheels horizontally into rivers or streams. The weight of the water in the buckets turned the wheel to power large circular stones that ground wheat into flour.

The Romans also used water wheels to grind grain, but placed them vertically into the water. Around 300 CE, the Romans built a huge flour mill in France.

The mill had 16 water wheels and produced enough flour to make bread for the 12,500 residents of the area. Historians call the mill the most powerful mechanical structure in the ancient world.

SIMPLE MACHINES!

GEAR WHEELS

A gear wheel has small teeth around the outside. Gear wheels always work in pairs. The teeth of one wheel fit perfectly into the teeth of the other wheel.

When one gear wheel moves, it passes along its motion and force to the second gear wheel. It's like a never-ending game of hot potato! Depending on how gears are put together, they can control how fast or slow an object moves.

FERRIS WHEELS

The wheel and axle can also provide fun entertainment—have you ever been on a Ferris wheel? From the 1600s, children in Europe and the Near East rode in seats hung from a wheel. These pleasure wheels were made of wood—and had to be turned by hand! In 1893, engineer George Washington Gale Ferris Jr. (1859–1896) built the first steam-powered wheel for the Chicago World's Fair. George wanted to build something that would amaze visitors to the fair. The 250-foot-high wheel had 36 hanging gondolas and could carry as many as 2,160 people. Today's Ferris wheels are even larger. The Ain Dubai is scheduled to open in 2019. At more than 668 feet tall, it will be the world's largest Ferris wheel, with 48 air-conditioned capsules!

Bicycle gears make it easier for you to climb up a hill or zoom down. If you have a bicycle, look at it. Do you see the gear wheels? When you switch gears on your bicycle, it changes how hard or easy it is to pedal. When your bike chain is wrapped around a large gear wheel, it is easier to push the pedals.

DID YOU KNOW?

The Tour de France was first held in 1903 and has since become the most famous cycling race in the world! This race takes three weeks to complete and covers more than 2,000 miles.

You're not doing much work, but your bicycle only moves a short distance. When the chain is wrapped around a smaller gear wheel, it takes more work to push the pedals. But your bicycle travels farther.

Simple machines are often related to each other, as wheels and axles are related to levers. In the next chapter, we'll learn about a simple machine related to the inclined plane—the screw!

? CONSIDER AND DISCUSS

It's time to consider and discuss: How is force transferred between the wheel and the axle?

PS The bicycle is a fun invention that uses the wheel and axle. **Watch this video to learn how bicycles have developed.**

KEYWORD PROMPTS

YouTube history bicycle dw 🔍

MOVING WITH ROLLERS

Ancient builders moved heavy stones with rollers. Discover how rollers work like wheels.

1 Start a scientific method worksheet and write a prediction in your science journal. How will pencil rollers affect the tray's movement?

2 Place several books on the tray. Place the tray on the ground. Using only two fingers, try to push the tray from one end of a room to another. Write your observations down in your science journal.

3 Space out the pencils until they are approximately the same length as the tray. Place the tray of books on the pencils.

4 Using only two fingers, try to push the tray from one end of a room to another. Hint: Keep moving the last pencil to the front. Write your observations in your science journal.

THINK ABOUT IT! What force did you use to move the tray across the floor? How is a roller different from a wheel and axle? Can you turn the tray using rollers? Record your observations in your science journal.

MAKE A SPINNING TOP

A spinning top is an example of a wheel and axle. The bottom of the top is the wheel and the spindle is the axle. The top spins when you turn the axle.

1 Measure a 3-by-1-inch rectangle on each piece of paper. Cut out the two rectangles.

2 Take one rectangle and fold the corner to the opposite edge to create a triangle. Do the same at the bottom. The square in the center should be about 1 inch. Repeat for the other rectangle.

3 Center the squares by placing one rectangle sheet across the other. Fold all the corners into the middle of the square. Secure the last fold by tucking it inside.

4 Poke a small hole in the center and insert the toothpick. The square should be closer to one end of the toothpick than the other.

5 Add a piece of clay to the toothpick end closest to the square. Stand the pointy end on a table, hold the top by the clay and give it a spin. It may take a few tries to get the hang of it—don't give up!

TRY THIS! Think about how you can spin your top faster. What else could you use to make a top? Have a contest with a few friends.

GEARING UP

When several gears are put together, they form a gear train. In this experiment, build and test your own gears.

IMPORTANT: Ask an adult to help you with the knife.

1 Thinly slice the potato to create two large wheels and one smaller wheel. The larger wheels should be about 3½ inches across.

2 Push an equal number of toothpicks into the rims of the two large slices, spacing them at regular intervals.

3 Push a paper fastener through the center of each wheel. Use two paper fasteners to secure the two large slices to the top of the shoebox lid. The toothpicks must fit together.

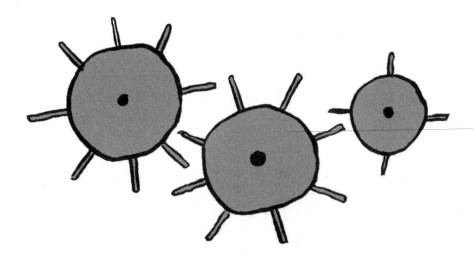

4 Gently turn one gear and watch what happens. Write your observations in your science journal.

5 Push half the number of toothpicks into the rim of the smaller wheel. Replace one of the large wheels with the smaller potato wheel. The toothpicks must fit together.

6 With a pen, mark one place on the wheel where the toothpick gears touch. Turn the larger wheel. Count how many times the smaller wheel rotates for a single rotation of the larger wheel. Write your observations in your science journal.

WHAT'S HAPPENING? Gears do different jobs depending on their size and how they are grouped. A large gear turning a smaller gear produces more speed. A small gear turning a larger gear produces more power. How do the teeth on the potato wheels work together? In what direction do the gears spin?

TRY THIS! Did you know that a rolling pin is a wheel and axle? The handles are the axle and the cylinder that rolls out the dough is the wheel. Try this easy experiment with dough and a rolling pin to find out how a wheel and axle can make work easier. Take one half of your dough and press it flat using only your hands. Now, take the other half and roll it flat with the rolling pin. Was it easier to flatten the dough with a wheel and axle? Can you name some other kitchen tools that have a wheel and axle?

CHAPTER 5

SCREWS

Screws are in objects all around you. The bottom of a light bulb is a screw. The chair you're sitting on has screws. Do you have a guitar? You turn a screw to tune it and make it sound good. Some screws hold objects together. Surgeons use metal screws to fix broken bones. The screws hold the bones in place until the injury is healed. Look around the room you are in. How many screws can you find?

A screw is a simple machine with an inclined plane wrapped around a cylinder. The inclined plane allows the screw to move in a circular pattern and pull one thing toward another.

WORDS to KNOW

screw: an inclined plane or lever wrapped around a pole that pulls one thing toward another.

thread: the raised edge of a screw that winds around.

pitch: the distance between the threads in a screw.

A screw looks like a nail with grooves around it, called threads. These are like a winding slide or spiral staircase. The distance between the threads is called the pitch. The threads wind evenly around the body of a screw. Because of the threads, screws hold on tightly and cannot easily be pulled out.

A person or a machine must turn a screw for it to work. Think of the bottle in your lunch kit. It probably has a screw lid. If you don't screw it tight enough, the bottle leaks— not good! All lids that you must turn to open or close are screws. Some screws have a notch at the top for a screwdriver. By turning the screwdriver, you push in and tighten or loosen the screw.

DID YOU KNOW?

When a screw's threads are close together, it takes more turns to tighten or loosen it. To find out how many turns it will take to twist a screw all the way in, count the threads!

TYPES OF SCREWS

Screws are very important in the world! There are a few different kinds of screws that perform different functions. Let's take a look.

Bolt: The strongest type of screw is a bolt. Unlike other screws, a bolt does not cut into the material being fastened. Instead, it goes through a hole in the material and is held in place by a nut on the other side.

Both the bolt and the nut have threads, just like a regular screw, so they fit tightly together. Bolts are used to join machinery and furniture.

Worm Gear: A worm gear is a type of screw with two parts—a worm and a worm wheel. The threads of the worm fit against a toothed wheel as they rotate.

WHAT TYPE OF THREAD CAN'T BE USED FOR SEWING?

A screw thread.

Worm gears are used in complex machines such as cars and trucks. Stringed instruments such as violins or cellos also use worm gears to keep them in tune. When the musician turns a knob attached to the worm gears, the gears move, tightening the string.

Drill Bit: Have you ever seen one of your parents use an electric drill? The drill holds a cutting tool called a drill bit, which spins very fast. The drill bit is pointed at one end and its edges have threads just like a screw. As the drill bit turns, pieces of material such as wood or metal are pulled up the threads and out of the hole being drilled.

Drill bits come in different shapes and sizes depending on the job they do. They cut holes into wood, metal, stone, and plastic.

HOW SCREWS CAN LIFT

The screw jack is a simple machine that can lift and support heavy things such as a piece of machinery or even a house! The jack has a strong screw that comes out of a base at the bottom. The jack goes under the object being lifted and the surface at the top of the jack supports the weight.

The most common type of screw jack is used to lift up a car to fix a flat tire. How does a screw jack work? With help from another simple machine—the lever.

··· DID YOU KNOW? ···

At 57-feet wide, a drill bit called Bertha was the largest in the world. Engineers in Seattle, Washington, used Bertha to dig a highway more than 1½ miles long under the city. It took the massive drill four years to finish the job, partly because it got stuck for a couple of years!

clockwise: in the direction the hands of a clock move.

WORDS ⊚ KNOW

First, you insert a metal bar into the jack, and then you turn the bar clockwise. This turning makes the screw rise out of the base. Whatever is resting on top of the jack is pushed upward.

THE ARCHIMEDES' SCREW

Around 250 BCE, Greek scientist Archimedes created an amazing new machine with a screw. His machine didn't hold objects together—it pumped water!

Archimedes' machine had a large screw inside a hollow tube. People placed one end of the tube into water and turned a crank. The crank caused the screw to turn, and the water at the bottom was brought up the tube along the turning spiral. Compared to hoisting up buckets of water by hand, the Archimedes' screw moved water with a lot less work.

AN ARCHIMEDES' SCREW IN ENGLAND
CREDIT: CHRISTOPHER DOWN (CC BY 4.0)

THEN & NOW

THEN: In ancient times, the Archimedes' screw pumped water from rivers or canals to fields.

NOW: Archimedes' screws the size of pencil erasers are used to keep blood pumping during heart surgery.

Today, we have new ways to pump water, but the Archimedes' screw is still being used in many places. For example, SeaWorld Adventure Park in San Diego, California, uses two Archimedes' screws to lift water for one of its rides.

One of the main uses for screws is to hold things together. In the next chapter, we'll learn about a simple machine that drives things apart—the wedge!

CONSIDER AND DISCUSS

It's time to consider and discuss: How does the screw help you to do work?

THE ROBERTSON SCREW

In 1908, Peter Lymburner Robertson (1879–1951) created a screw with a very deep, square opening on the head. He also designed a screwdriver with a square end to fit securely in his new screw. Because the screwdriver didn't slip out, people could use the screwdriver with one hand. This helped them to work faster. Soon, big companies such as the Ford Motor Company were using Peter's design. The Model T car made by Ford used more than 700 Robertson screws! These screws are still popular today.

MAKE A JACK

Did you know that screws can be used to lift heavy objects? While small jacks can lift only the corner of a car, larger screw jacks can lift an entire vehicle.

1 Using scissors, take one of the plastic lids and make a hole in the middle. It should be slightly larger than the **diameter** of the bolt.

2 Insert the bolt into the hole from the underside of the lid and secure with tape. This piece should be able to stand on a flat surface.

3 Make a hole in the middle of the second lid. This lid will face up to form your platform. Place the nut under the hole and secure with tape. Do not put tape over the center.

4 Place the bottom lid (with the bolt) on a flat surface and twist the nut in the second lid **counterclockwise** onto the bolt. Record your observations in your science journal. Now twist the nut clockwise. What happens?

THINK ABOUT IT! Do you need to apply gentle force or strong force to turn the screw? Where would this type of machine be helpful?

WORDS ⊙ KNOW

diameter: the distance across a circle through the middle.

counterclockwise: in the opposite direction to the way the hands of a clock move.

PROJECT!

LET'S DO THE TWIST

Complex machines need screws, nuts, and bolts to hold them together. Try this activity to discover why screws are stronger than nails.

SUPPLIES

* hammer
* nail
* block of wood
* screwdriver
* screw
* science journal

> **IMPORTANT:** Have an adult supervise the use of tools.

1 In your science journal, start a scientific method worksheet and write a prediction. Is there an advantage to using a screw instead of a nail? Why?

2 Using the hammer, pound the nail into the block of wood. Now, use the screwdriver to insert the screw into the block.

3 Remove the nail from the wood using the end of the hammer. Try to remove the screw from the wood using the end of the hammer.

4 Record your observations in your science journal.

WHAT'S HAPPENING?

Friction holds the nail and screw in place. By gripping the wood, the screw's threads allow it to resist friction better. While a nail can be pulled directly out of the wood, a screw must be turned.

  An American artist named Andrew Myers makes amazing portraits entirely out of screws. **Watch this video to learn more about Andrew's art.**

KEYWORD PROMPTS

Cantor Vimeo Myers screw art

SUPPLIES

* paper
* ruler
* scissors
* paper clip

MAKE A MINI-HELICOPTER

The blades of a helicopter are a powerful screw. They can lift it off the ground. Try this activity to learn how helicopter blades act like a screw.

1 Measure and cut out a strip of paper 5 inches long and ½ inch wide. Fold the paper in half and put a paper clip on the folded edge, just three-quarters of the way on.

2 Fold the top wings down at an angle. They should stick out slightly.

3 Hold the helicopter by the paper clip. Stand on a chair or at the top of a staircase and drop it. What happens? Which way does the helicopter spin, clockwise or counterclockwise?

TRY THIS! Change the size of the blades. Will the length of the blades affect how long the helicopter can stay in the air?

LEONARDO DA VINCI

Leonardo da Vinci (1452–1519) was an artist and an inventor who kept notebooks filled with his ideas. He drew a flying machine that looked like a helicopter, 500 years before the first one was built! Leonardo's sketches inspired engineer Igor I. Sikorsky (1889–1972) to begin working on helicopter designs in the early 1900s. Sikorsky helicopters are still made today.

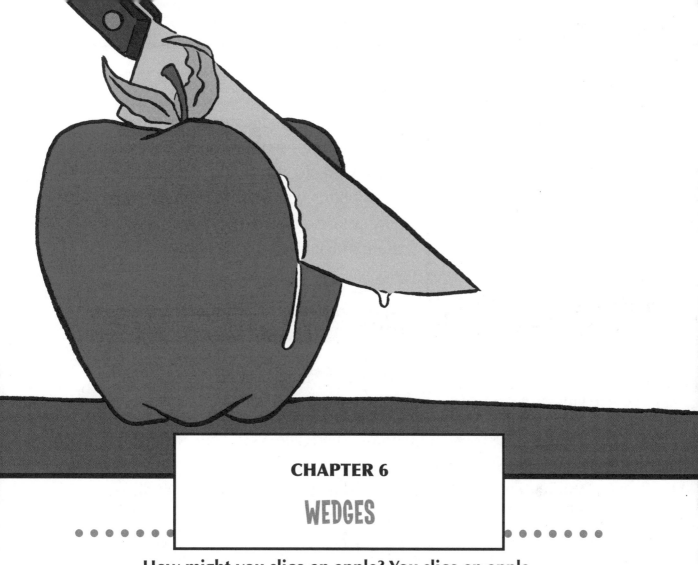

CHAPTER 6

WEDGES

How might you slice an apple? You slice an apple by pushing down on a knife. The knife takes your downward force and turns it into a sideways force. What's another term for your knife? A wedge!

A wedge is a simple machine with two inclined planes that end in a sharp point. One end of the wedge is thicker than the other end. Wedges do more than just push objects apart. We use wedges called the blades of a pair of scissors to cut an object into smaller pieces.

?  **INVESTIGATE!**

How does a wedge separate two objects?

WORDS TO KNOW

wedge: an object with slanted sides ending in a sharp edge that lifts or splits another object.

sculptor: a person who uses materials such as stone or clay to produce practical objects or works of art.

mallet: a hammer with a flat wood or rubber end.

We also use wedges to stop objects from moving—a doorstop! A doorstop is an example of a single wedge. It has one sloping side, and its thinnest part goes under a door to hold it still. Axes, thumb tacks, scissors, and nails are also wedges.

SINGLES AND DOUBLES

There are two kinds of wedges. A single wedge has one sloping side and a double wedge has two sloping sides.

Many sculptors and woodworkers use a single wedge called a chisel to shape stone, wood, or even ice. First, they push the thinner end of the chisel into the material they wish to shape. Then, they tap on the opposite end of the chisel with a mallet to cause the material to separate. In this way, artists carve fantastic shapes and designs.

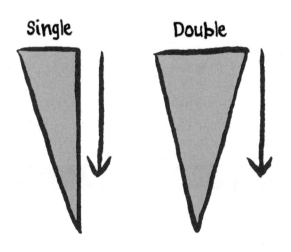

Single   Double

Double wedges such as knives, shovels, and axes have two sloping sides. People use double wedges to split, fasten, or cut. For example, a person raises an axe and then strikes the wood below, using downward force. The sharp end of the axe splits the wood apart—the downward force is pushed outward.

THEN: To clear a road after a snowstorm, horses dragged wooden wedge plows through the snow.

NOW: Snowplows are equipped with large, metal wedges on the front. These wedges push the snow to the side of the road to clear a path for vehicles.

The end of a nail is also a double wedge. The point makes an opening for the wider part of the nail to enter. When the wider body of the nail goes into the opening, it pushes apart material such as wood. That makes it easier for the nail to go deeper.

Some wedges are a part of our bodies. For example, teeth are a type of wedge you use to bite and chew with. Other types of wedges are made by people. Let's find out more about human-made wedges!

WEDGE HISTORY

Early people made wedges out of wood, bone, and shell. For example, they altered stone by taking a hard stone and using it to hammer a softer stone into the shape they wanted. Hammering away at the sides of the softer stone created sharp edges—in this way, people made a wedge-shaped tool.

These early wedges were used for cutting, scraping, splitting, and digging. They were also used as weapons. Hunters attached wedges to the ends of sticks to make spears and arrowheads. After they killed an animal, they used the wedges for cutting and scraping the meat from the skin.

61

Native American tribes such as the Paiute used wedges to hunt, trap, and fish. For example, they made arrowheads from a glass-like stone called obsidian. To carve the arrowhead, the Paiute used another wedge made from the tip of a deer antler. They had to chip away at the obsidian with the antler until it formed an arrowhead.

The Paiute attached the arrowhead to a long stick to create a tool called an atlatl. A hunter threw the atlatl when hunting large animals such as deer.

SNOW SNAKE

Snow snake is a winter sport. It has been played in North America since before European settlers arrived. Indigenous people, including the Ojibwe in what is now Wisconsin, still play snow snake. A snow snake is a beautifully carved pole. Poles vary in length, but most are between 3 and 6 feet long. The snow snake is an example of a third-class lever. The tip of the snow snake is carved into a point, or a wedge. The Ojibwe carve their snow snakes from wood. Some indigenous people, including the Sioux, traditionally used bones. To play, the player holds the snow snake in one hand. The sharp end of the snow snake points in the direction the player wants it to travel. The player flings the snow snake underhand down a flat, slippery track. The player whose snow snake travels the farthest is the winner.

PUSHING AND SUPPORTING

We learned how the ancient Egyptians used different simple machines, such as inclined planes, to build pyramids. They also used wedges to split giant stone blocks. First, they chipped away at the stone with a chisel. Then, they pushed wooden wedges into the crack.

Workers poured water into the crack to make the wedges swell. The wedges pushed the crack apart, making it easier for workers to cut the stone down to size.

Ancient Romans used wedges, too. In addition to using wedges as hand tools, the

DID YOU KNOW?

One of the narrowest houses in the world is in Scotland. The home is only 47 inches wide at the front. There's just enough room for a front door! The home is nicknamed "the Wedge" because it gets wider toward the back.

Romans made wedge-shaped blocks of stone to build arches in buildings and bridges.

Roman engineers realized that arches could support more weight than a simple stack of blocks. Each wedge-shaped block had to fit together perfectly. During construction, the center stone was added last. It is called the keystone because it is the key to holding the arch! Some of these Roman structures still stand today. And the Roman arch is still being used by engineers today.

WHAT DID THE APPLE SAY TO THE WEDGE?

You split me up!

THERE ARE WEDGES IN THE KEYSTONE ARCHES OF THE ROMAN COLOSSEUM, BUILT IN THE FIRST CENTURY CE.

EVERYDAY WEDGES

The wedge has many different jobs. Staples are wedges that hold sheets of paper together. A shovel is a wedge you use to move snow or to build a giant sandcastle at the beach.

When you zip up your coat, you're using wedges, too. A zipper has wedges on either side of the slider. They line up the teeth and push them together. When the slider is pulled down, the wedges pull apart the teeth.

Many of the wedges you use are in the kitchen. Have you ever helped make pancakes? Pancakes can't flip themselves—you need a spatula to lift each hot pancake.

The head of the spatula is a wedge and the handle is a lever. The spatula's head is actually two inclined planes. To use the spatula, you slide the narrow part of the wedge under the pancake and apply a pushing force to the lever. The force moves down the spatula and up and over your pancake.

Useful wedges don't end at the stove. You use a wedge to eat most of your meals—a fork! The wedges on the fork are the long points, or tines, on the end. The tines help you break apart your food.

We've looked at five different simple machines so far. We have one more to go, and in the next chapter we'll learn about the pulley!

CONSIDER AND DISCUSS

It's time to consider and discuss: How does a wedge separate two objects?

FARMING WITH WEDGES

For thousands of years, farmers worked the land with a type of wedge called a plow. Farm animals pulled the plow. It loosened the soil so seeds could be planted more easily. John Deere (1804–1886) was a pioneer and inventor from Vermont. In 1837, John invented the steel walking plow. He made it from the steel of a broken saw blade. The strong blade made it possible for farmers to plow the dense soil of North America's Midwest. John sold his plow across America. Today, his company still sells farm equipment.

SUPPLIES

* ✳ science journal
* ✳ banana
* ✳ apple
* ✳ bread roll

EATING WITH WEDGES

Smile wide and say "cheese." You just showed your wedges! Investigate how teeth are a type of wedge. Which of your teeth do you bite with? Chew with?

1 Write a prediction in your science journal. Which teeth do you think will be easier to bite with and why?

2 Take a bite of banana. Write down in your journal which teeth you used. Repeat with the apple. Now bite into the roll.

CHOMP

3 Look at your results and compare them to your prediction.

WHAT'S HAPPENING?

Your teeth help to break down food into smaller pieces. The teeth in the front of your mouth look like narrow wedges. Narrow wedges cut more easily than wider wedges. The teeth at the back of your mouth are called molars. They are wide wedges good for grinding up food. Can you identify another body part that is like a wedge? Write down this body part in your science journal and explain why it is a wedge.

LET'S CARVE FRUIT

A knife is a wedge that helps you push apart things, such as food. In this activity, you will turn a banana into a dolphin with the help of a knife.

SUPPLIES

* banana
* cutting board
* small plastic knife
* plate
* kiwi
* raisins

IMPORTANT: Have an adult help you with the knife.

1 Peel the banana. Slice the bottom off the banana so it can rest flat. Keep this slice. Put the banana on the plate.

2 Use the knife to cut out a wedge on the front for the dolphin's mouth. Keep the wedge you cut out.

3 Make a slit in the top toward the front of the dolphin and insert the mouth wedge to make a top fin.

4 Make a slit at the tail end and insert the slice you cut from the belly. This will be the tail fin.

5 Peel the kiwi and cut it into slices ¼-inch thick. Cut one slice in half for the dorsal fins of the dolphin. You can simply prop these up against the banana. Add raisins on top for the eyes.

6 Arrange the rest of the kiwi around your plate for the waves. Now, your banana dolphin is ready to eat.

TRY THIS! Carve more creatures with other fruits and vegetables.

TESTING A WEDGE

The front of a boat is shaped to be a wedge. Imagine if the front of a boat was square. How would the boat move differently through the water?

1 Write a prediction in your science journal. Do you think it will be easier to pull the boat from its pointed front, called the bow, or from its flat end, the stern?

2 Place the carton sideways on a table with the opening facing up. Use a ruler and a pencil to mark the halfway point (lengthwise) on the container. Cut the container in half.

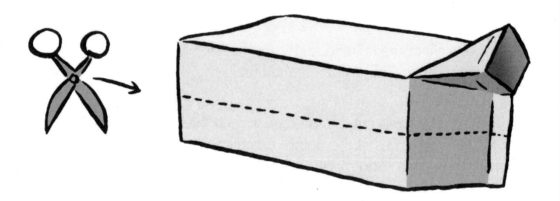

3 Cover the outside of the boat with masking tape. Use the markers to create a design on the tape. You can give your boat a name.

4 Attach a piece of string to the back of the boat with tape. How will this affect how the boat moves through the water? Write down a prediction in your science journal.

5 Try to pull the boat through a tub of water. Write down your observations in your science journal.

6 Now, attach the string to the bow of the boat, or the front. How will this affect how the boat moves through the water? Write down a prediction in your science journal. Pull your boat through the water. Compare your results.

THINK ABOUT IT! Which way was it easier to pull the boat through the water? How would you describe the movement of the water when the boat was pulled by the bow compared to when it was pulled by the stern?

SUGAR CUBE CHALLENGE

Explore how wedges can be used to separate objects.

1 Write a prediction in your science journal. Will a wedge or a block make it easier to split a sugar cube wall apart and why?

2 Use 10 sugar cubes to make a mini-wall. Divide the sugar cubes into two stacks. Each stack should have five cubes.

3 Slide a few hair ties around the wall of sugar cubes to push them closer together.

4 Take the extra sugar cube and press it gently on top of the wall where the two stacks meet. Is the sugar cube able to separate the stacks? Write down your results in your science journal.

5 Use the sharp end of the pencil as a wedge. Repeat step 4. What happens?

DID YOU KNOW?

Pont du Gard is a 2,000-year-old arch bridge in Avignon, France. Roman engineers built the bridge between 20 and 16 BCE to bring water to the people of the nearby city of Nimes. The bridge ran for 31 miles! The bridge has three separate tiers. There are six arches on the lowest tier, 11 arches in the middle, and 35 small arches at the top!

THINK ABOUT IT! Which tool made it easier to separate the sugar cube stacks? Why do you think this was?

CHAPTER 7

PULLEYS

You see pulleys in lots of different places. Tow trucks use pulleys to lift broken-down cars and trucks. Have you ever watched the flag being raised at your school? No one climbs to the top of the pole with the flag. Instead, they use a pulley to raise and lower the flag each morning and evening.

A pulley has a wheel with two raised sides. A rope or chain sits in the groove. The edges of the wheel keep the rope from sliding out. Pulleys let you lift and lower loads with ease. Do you have blinds on your windows? Pulleys move them up and down. Some clotheslines have pulleys at either end so you can move the clothes away from or toward you.

? | **INVESTIGATE!**

How is a pulley useful?

pulley: a wheel with a grooved rim that a rope or chain is pulled through to help lift a load.

fixed pulley: a pulley that is joined to a point that does not move.

movable pulley: a pulley that moves together with the load.

WORDS TO KNOW

Ski slopes use pulleys, too. A rope tow is a simple pulley. It is a rope strung between two wheels that pulls beginner skiers or children up small hills.

Pulleys are also found on construction sites and in ports. Cranes use pulleys and levers to lift loads such as beams for building. Cranes also lift objects such as trucks and cars and shipping containers.

There are two basic types of pulleys—fixed and movable. Let's take a look at how these both work.

FIXED PULLEY

A fixed pulley is attached to a structure such as a post or a wall. A flagpole uses a fixed pulley. The pulley at the top of the pole does not move. When someone pulls on the rope around the pulley's wheel, the rope moves, but the pulley does not.

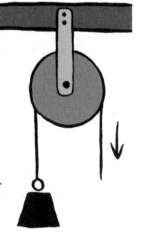

Have you ever opened window blinds? Then you have used a fixed pulley. A long cord wraps around a pulley wheel at the top of the blinds. You hold on to the end of the cord. When you pull down on the cord, the blinds rise. You can see outside!

A fixed pulley does not increase the force being used. It only changes the direction of a force. People use fixed pulleys because they make the job of lifting an object easier.

THEN: Pulleys relied on people power, water wheels, and steam engines to make them turn.

NOW: Pulley systems in modern machinery, such as cranes, rely on motorized engines.

MOVABLE PULLEY

A movable pulley is not fixed in one place. Its wheel moves along the rope. In this type of pulley, one end of the rope is fixed to an object such as a hook above the load. The load is attached to the end of the pulley that moves. When you pull on the rope, the rope moves across a longer distance, but you use less force.

A zip-line is a movable pulley. A simple zip-line runs on a slope. A metal cable connects a higher platform to a lower one. Riders sit in a harness that is directly attached to the pulley. When they push off from the higher platform, gravity pulls them down the cable.

SIMPLE MACHINES!

TOGETHER IS BETTER

When a fixed and movable pulley are used together, they make a compound pulley. A compound pulley allows you to lift a heavy object and change the direction of a force at the same time.

Sailors use compound pulleys on their sailboats. A rope connected to a sail is wound through several pulleys. Out on the water, sailors pull on the rope to raise the sail. The wind fills the sail and pushes the boat along.

PULLEYS IN HISTORY

Around 1500 BCE, farmers in the Middle East began using pulleys. Pulleys made it easier for farmers to lift water for their crops.

People also needed safe water to drink, so they dug deep water wells. They hung a wooden pulley wheel from a pole above the well. A rope wrapped around the wheel had a long-necked pot tied to it. To lift the filled pot, people tugged on the rope.

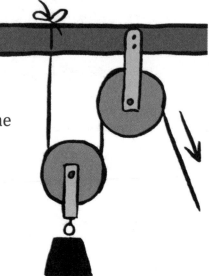

·· DID YOU KNOW? ··

You use pulleys to tie your shoes. The tiny holes on your shoes are movable pulleys. When you tug on the laces, the pulleys move closer together. Now your shoes won't fall off!

A BASKET ELEVATOR

In the thirteenth century, workers built the Abbey of Mont St. Michel at the top of a 260-foot rock off the coast of Normandy, France. Walking up the steep road to the abbey was hard work, so workers built an elevator. The elevator looked like a large basket. To raise the basket, donkeys pulled on the rope of a pulley that wound round a wooden wheel and the basket lifted. It carried people and supplies to the top.

In time, improvements were made to the design. Some pulley chains were made with bronze, making them much stronger.

The Romans used cranes to build large structures. Some of their larger cranes used up to five pulleys. A massive treadwheel was used to power their cranes. Workers, mostly slaves, walked within the wheel to make the pulleys move. It looked like a giant hamster wheel!

(PS) **Watch engineers build a model of a Colosseum elevator.**
Why was the trapdoor a challenge for engineers to design?

KEYWORD PROMPTS
PBS learning construct model Colosseum 🔍

SIMPLE MACHINES!

THE RUINS OF THE ROMAN COLOSSEUM

In 70 CE, the Romans began building a large arena for gladiator games in Rome, Italy. Romans came to the Colosseum to watch people and wild animals—including lions, tigers, and bears—fight.

The Colosseum had simple elevators that used pulleys. Animals and gladiators were kept in the basement until showtime, when they rode elevators up to the fighting floor.

From levers to pulleys, simple machines are the basic tools people use to build and power the world. When you think like an engineer and figure out ways to design new things using simple machines, you can come up with amazing ideas that have never been tried!

Take what you've learned in this book and use your engineering knowledge to find ways of making the world a better place. Maybe you'll invent a machine that converts used plastic bottles into life-saving devices. Maybe you'll figure out how to better equip a classroom for use by people with ability challenges. Whatever your goal, simple machines are sure to be part of the solution!

 CONSIDER AND DISCUSS

It's time to consider and discuss: How is a pulley useful?

CREATE A FIXED PULLEY

How do fixed pulleys help people to lift and move objects? Try this activity and see.

SUPPLIES

* ✳ science journal
* ✳ water bottle
* ✳ water
* ✳ 2 empty yogurt containers with lids
* ✳ tape
* ✳ scissors
* ✳ string
* ✳ wooden skewer

1 Start a scientific method worksheet and write a prediction in your science journal. Is it easier to lift a water bottle with or without a pulley?

2 Fill the water bottle half full with water. Pick up the water bottle with one hand and set it back down. Write down your observations in your science journal.

3 To make a pulley wheel, tape the yogurt container to the center of one lid. Tape the second lid to the other side of the container. This is the wheel of your pulley.

4 Push the end of the scissors carefully through the center of the wheel. Push the skewer through this hole so it turns easily. Balance the skewer between the backs of two chairs.

5 Place the water bottle on the floor directly beneath the skewer. Tie one end of the string around the neck of the bottle. Loop the other end of the string over the pulley wheel. Pull on the string.

6 Write your observations in your science journal and compare them to your prediction.

THINK ABOUT IT!

How does the pulley change the direction of your force? In what direction did you pull? In what direction did the water bottle move?

77

CREATE A MOVABLE PULLEY

A construction crane is a movable pulley. The pulley and the load move together. Try this activity to see how a movable pulley works.

1 Carefully poke a hole 1½ inches down each side of your container with scissors.

2 Thread a piece of string through the holes. Tie knots in each end to form a small handle.

3 Tape the magnet to the bottom of the container with clear tape. Set this to one side.

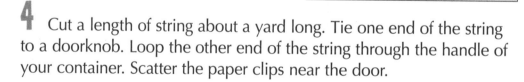

4 Cut a length of string about a yard long. Tie one end of the string to a doorknob. Loop the other end of the string through the handle of your container. Scatter the paper clips near the door.

5 Pull on the string to pick up the paper clips. What happens? Where does the load go when the pulley moves?

TRY THIS! Add the pulley wheel from the first activity to make a compound pulley. Ask a partner to hold onto the skewer of the pulley wheel and rest one end of the skewer on a doorknob. Loop the thread from the moving pulley over the wheel. Pull down on the string. Does the compound pulley make your work easier? If so, how?

A PULLEY RELAY

See which team can move all its golf balls from the bottom of a play structure or treehouse to the top first!

SUPPLIES

* 4 people
* play structure
* 2 ropes
* 4 pails
* about 20 golf balls

1 Make up teams of two people each. Decide who will be at the top of the play structure and who will remain at the bottom. You can take turns.

2 Each team gets a rope and two pails. Tie the rope to one of the pails. Then loop the rope over a beam of the play structure. Place the other pail at the top of the structure to collect the golf balls.

3 Each team begins with the same number of the golf balls. Put them into two piles at the bottom of the play structure.

4 Everyone gets into position. When both teams are ready, have someone yell "Go." The person at the bottom of the pulley places one golf ball in the pail and pulls down on the rope to raise the pail. The player at the top removes the golf ball and places it in the empty pail. The player on the ground then lowers the pail to the ground.

5 Repeat these steps until one team moves all its golf balls to the top of the structure. The team that does this first, wins!

SUPPLIES

* 16-ounce milk or cream container
* scissors
* ruler
* yarn
* tape
* pencil

CREATE A DRAWBRIDGE

Some castles had a drawbridge to control who came in or out of the castle. Pulleys allowed the drawbridge to be raised or lowered. Try this activity to see how this worked.

1 Cut the back off the carton. In the middle of the front of the carton, draw a rectangle 5 by 6 inches. This will be the drawbridge. Carefully cut out the top and sides of your drawbridge. Do not cut along the bottom.

2 Cut two 15-inch pieces of yarn. Tape one end of each piece to the top of the drawbridge. About 1 inch above the opening on the carton, poke two holes through the carton and thread the other ends of the yarn pieces through them.

3 On the sides of the container, mark the halfway point between the front and back. The marks should be at the same height as the holes on the front.

4 Make holes at these marks. Push the pencil through the holes. Wrap each piece of yarn around the pencil once.

•••• DID YOU KNOW? ••••••

Have you ever seen an old-fashioned well? Many of these have buckets hanging from pulleys! This simple machine helped people haul heavy water from deep underground.

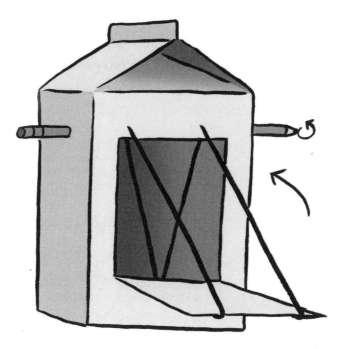

5 Now, make a hole in the center of the bottom piece of the carton, below the drawbridge.

6 Thread both pieces of yarn through this hole. Tie the two pieces of yarn together with a knot. Twist the pencil to raise or lower the drawbridge.

THINK ABOUT IT!
What modern structures use drawbridges?

DESIGN A NEW INVENTION

Try this activity to design, make, and test a new invention using simple machines. This activity is fun to do alone or in a group.

1 Decide what task your machine will accomplish and where your machine will be used, such as a kitchen, office, or playground.

2 Sketch your design in your journal. Label each simple machine in your design.

3 Now, assemble all the materials you will need to build your machine. Construct your invention and test out your design.

·· DID YOU KNOW? ·······

Rube Goldberg (1883-1970) was an engineer, cartoonist, and author. As a cartoonist, he was famous for pictures of extraordinary "inventions" that used a chain reaction to turn a simple task into a complicated one. Rube's inventions used simple machines, including wheels, levers, and pulleys.

4 Take note of what doesn't work, redesign, and test again.

TRY THIS! Work in a group to solve a real-life problem in the world, such as climate change, poverty, bullying, or something else. How can you use simple machines to build a device that will help people?

archaeologist: a scientist who studies ancient people through the objects they left behind.

atlatl: a wooden hunting tool used by some Native people in North America.

axle: a rod on which a wheel rotates.

bar: the part of a lever that balances the weight of an object and applies the force to move that object.

BCE: put after a date, BCE stands for Before Common Era and counts down to zero. CE stands for Common Era and counts up from zero. This book was printed in 2019 CE.

canal: a long waterway made by people that moves water or is used for transportation.

catapult: a weapon used to throw heavy objects.

chariot: a two-wheeled, horse-drawn vehicle from ancient times, which was used in battle and in races.

chisel: a tool with a long handle and a sharp wedge.

clockwise: in the direction the hands of a clock move.

compound machine: two or more simple machines working together.

compound pulley: a fixed pulley and movable pulley working together.

counterclockwise: in the opposite direction to the way the hands of a clock move.

crops: plants grown for food and other uses.

cylinder: a hollow tube shape.

data: information gathered from tests or experiments.

diameter: the distance across a circle through the middle.

effort: the force that is used on a simple machine to move the load.

Egyptologist: a person who studies the ancient history and culture of Egypt.

engineer: someone who uses science, math, and creativity to design products or processes to meet human needs or solve problems.

equilibrium: balance between opposing forces.

fixed pulley: a pulley that is joined to a point that does not move.

force: a push or pull that changes an object's motion.

friction: a force that slows down objects when they rub against each other.

fulcrum: the point or support where a lever turns.

funicular: a type of mountainside railroad that uses cables attached to pulleys to move the train cars up and down.

gear: a toothed wheel or cylinder that connects with another toothed part to send motion from one rotating body to another.

gladiator: a person who was forced to fight for entertainment.

gravity: a force that pulls objects to the earth.

horizontal: straight across from side to side.

inclined plane: a sloped surface that connects a lower level to a higher level.

indigenous: native to a place.

International Space Station: a massive space station orbiting Earth where astronauts live, conduct experiments, and study space.

lever: a simple machine made of a rigid bar that pivots on a support, called a fulcrum.

linkage: a link that connects two or more levers together.

load: the object you are moving in your work.

lock: an enclosure in a canal with gates at each end used to raise or lower boats as they pass from one level to another.

lubricant: a substance, such as oil or grease, that reduces friction.

mallet: a hammer with a flat wood or rubber end.

mass: the amount of matter in an object.

mechanical advantage: something making work easier.

movable pulley: a pulley that moves together with the load.

newton: a unit used to measure the amount of force you need to move an object.

nut: a small metal fastener with screw threads on the inside.

orbit: the path an object in space takes around a star, planet, or moon.

pitch: the distance between the threads in a screw.

pivot: the fixed point—the fulcrum—supporting something that turns.

prototype: a working model of something that allows engineers to test their idea.

pulley: a wheel with a grooved rim that a rope or chain is pulled through to help lift a load.

quarry: a pit where stone is cut.

rotate: to turn around a fixed point.

screw: an inclined plane or lever wrapped around a pole that pulls one thing toward another.

sculptor: a person who uses materials such as stone or clay to produce practical objects or works of art.

shaduf: a water-lifting device.

simple machine: a tool with few or no moving parts that uses one movement to complete work. The six simple machines are the lever, inclined plane, wheel and axle, screw, wedge, and pulley.

skeleton: a winter sport in which a driver rides headfirst down a track on a sled.

spokes: bars or wire rods connecting the center of a wheel to the outside rim.

switchback: a road that zigzags up a steep hill or mountain.

thread: the raised edge of a screw that winds around.

tines: the sharp points at the end of a fork.

trade: the exchange of goods for other goods or money.

treadwheel: a wheel turned by an animal or a person.

vertical: straight up and down.

water wheel: a wheel with paddles attached that spins when water flows over it. The energy can be used to power machines or lift water.

wedge: an object with slanted sides ending in a sharp edge that lifts or splits another object.

wheel and axle: a wheel with a rod that turn together to lift and move loads. The axle is the rod around which the wheel rotates.

METRIC CONVERSIONS

Use this chart to find the metric equivalents to the English measurements in this book. If you need to know a half measurement, divide by two. If you need to know twice the measurement, multiply by two. How do you find a quarter measurement? How do you find three times the measurement?

English	Metric
1 inch	2.5 centimeters
1 foot	30.5 centimeters
1 yard	0.9 meter
1 mile	1.6 kilometers
1 pound	0.5 kilogram
1 teaspoon	5 milliliters
1 tablespoon	15 milliliters
1 cup	237 milliliters

BOOKS

Aronson, Sarah. *Just Like Rube Goldberg: The Incredible True Story of the Man Behind the Machines.* Beach Lane Books, 2019.

Klepeis, Alicia. *Explore Makerspace! With 25 Great Projects.* Nomad Press, 2017.

Long, Paul. *Build Your Own Chain Reaction Machines: How to Make Crazy Contraptions Using Everyday Stuff—Creative Kid-Powered Projects!* Quarry Books, 2018.

Macaulay, David. *The Way Things Work Now.* HMH Books for Young Readers, 2016.

Perdew, Laura. *Crazy Contraptions: Build Rube Goldberg Machines that Swoop, Spin, Stack, and Swivel: with Engineering Activities for Kids.* Nomad Press, 2019.

Rooney, Anne. *You Wouldn't Want to Live Without Simple Machines!* Franklin Watts, 2018.

WEBSITES

National Geographic Kids:
kids.nationalgeographic.com/kids

NOVA—Galileo Experiments:
pbs.org/wgbh/nova/galileo/experiments

PBS—The Design Squad:
pbskids.org/designsquad

California Science Center:
californiasciencecenter.org

MUSEUMS

Eli Whitney Museum and Workshop:
eliwhitney.org

Frost Science:
frostscience.org

Museum of the History of Science:
mhs.ox.ac.uk

The Carnegie Science Museum:
carnegiesciencecenter.org

The Exploratorium:
exploratorium.edu

The Museum of Science Industry Chicago:
msichicago.org

ESSENTIAL QUESTIONS

Introduction: What are simple machines? What are they used for?

Chapter 1: What is force? What is gravity? How do forces affect motion?

Chapter 2: How do levers change the strength of a force?

Chapter 3: How do inclined planes help people move objects?

Chapter 4: How is force transferred between the wheel and the axle?

Chapter 5: How does the screw help you to do work?

Chapter 6: How does a wedge separate two objects?

Chapter 7: How is a pulley useful?

QR CODE GLOSSARY

Page 2: bbc.com/education/topics/zvpp34j

Page 12: learnenglishkids.britishcouncil.org/en/short-stories/isaac-newton

Page 15: nces.ed.gov/nceskids/createagraph

Page 18: youtube.com/watch?time_continue=7&v=YlYEi0PgG1g

Page 21: asc-csa.gc.ca/eng/multimedia/games/canadarm2/default.asp

Page 31: youtube.com/watch?v=3_1Y8UoLIu4

Page 33: youtube.com/watch?v=q_Mddckb7Lg

Page 41: theguardian.com/science/2016/feb/19/archaeologists-excavate-bronze-age-wheel-cambridgeshire

Page 45: youtube.com/watch?v=yqkDW14S6JQ

Page 57: vimeo.com/166149898

Page 75: pbslearningmedia.org/resource/nvco-sci-constructingmodels/nova-building-wonders-colosseum-constructing-the-colosseum-with-models/#.WpsdH-jwZPY